26.097 Zei
inert, Karen.
e Amistad slave revolt
and American aboli$ 12.95

W9-BJR-479

The
Amistad
Slave Revolt
and
American Abolition

The *Amistad* Slave Revolt and American Abolition

by Karen Zeinert

LINNET BOOKS

1997

© 1997 Karen Zeinert.
All rights reserved.
First published 1997 as a Linnet Book,
an imprint of
The Shoe String Press, Inc.,
North Haven, CT 06473.

Library of Congress Cataloging-in-Publication Data

Zeinert, Karen.
The Amistad slave revolt and American abolition / Karen Zeinert.
p.   cm.
Includes bibliographical references and index.
Summary: Traces the 1839 revolt of Africans aboard the slave ship
Amistad, their apprehension, and long trial which ended in their
acquittal by the Supreme Court.
ISBN 0-208-02438-7 (cloth: alk. paper)
ISBN 0-208-02439-5 (paper: alk. paper)
1. Slavery—United States—Insurrections, etc.——Juvenile
literature.   2. Amistad (Schooner)—Juvenile literature.
3. Antislavery movements—United States—Juvenile literature.
[1. Amistad (Schooner)   2. Slavery—Insurrections.   3. Antislavery
movements.]   I. Title.
E447.Z45   1997
326'.0973—dc21   96-49021
                                                                    CIP
                                                                    AC

The paper in this publication meets the minimum requirements
of American National Standard for Information Sciences—
Permanence of Paper for Printed Library Materials,
ANSI Z39.48-1984.♾

Designed by Abigail Johnston
Printed in the United States of America

TO AMBER AND JASON

Contents

Editor's Note

SOME OF THE NAMES used in this text have a variety of spellings in reference books. For example, the leader of the rebellion on the *Amistad* is referred to as Singbe, Cinquez, and Cinque. Another African's name has been given as Foni, Fawni, and Fonne. The spellings chosen for this book are the ones most commonly used in published materials.

Contemporary African usage suggests that the man called Cinque was actually named Sengbe Pieh. The full name of the ship he commandeered with his African compatriots was *La Amistad*.

Introduction

I N 1839, FIFTY-THREE captive Africans aboard *La Amistad,* a ship bound for Puerto Príncipe, Cuba, revolted. After taking control of the ship, the blacks ordered two plantation owners, whose lives they had spared, to sail them to Africa. Instead, the cunning hostages slowly worked the ship into American waters and American history. It would take two long years before some of the Africans would once again see their beloved homeland, Mende country in Sierra Leone. These years were filled with extraordinary trials and triumphs. This is their story.

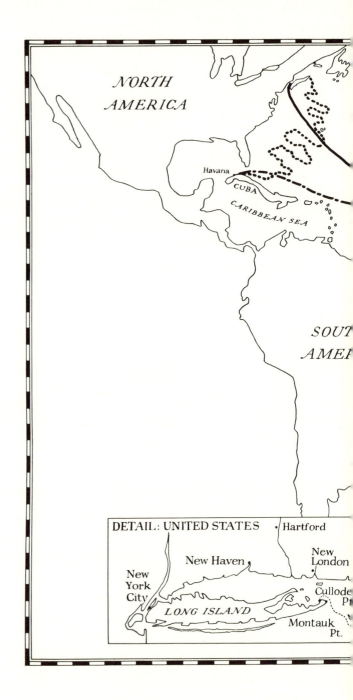

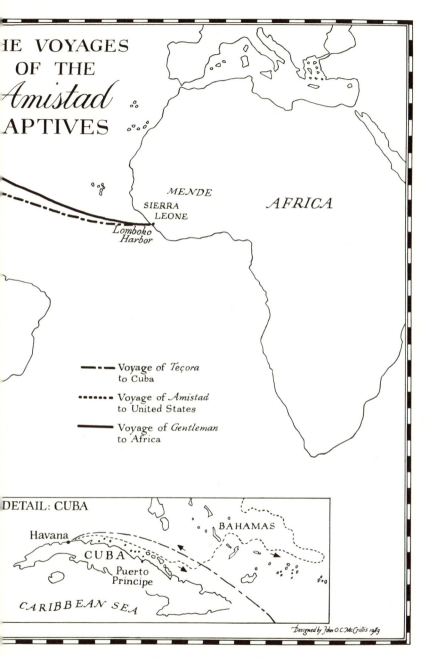

IE VOYAGES
OF THE
Amistad
APTIVES

MENDE

SIERRA
LEONE

AFRICA

Lomboko
Harbor

—·— Voyage of *Teçora*
to Cuba

······ Voyage of *Amistad*
to United States

—— Voyage of *Gentleman*
to Africa

DETAIL: CUBA

Havana

BAHAMAS

CUBA

Puerto
Principe

CARIBBEAN SEA

Designed by John O.C.McCrillis 1989

BY JOHN O.C. MCCRILLIS. Courtesy of the New Haven Colony Historical Society.

Timeline

1433   Portuguese seafarers round Cape Bojador on the west coast of Africa, probably the first Europeans to do so. They begin to explore the coast and discover a large native population.

1441   Portuguese sea captain Antam Goncalvez returns from exploring West Africa with two slaves, the first in Europe from this area.

1443   One of Goncalvez's men, Nuño Tristao, captures 235 slaves. This is the beginning of the Portuguese slave trade.

1492   Columbus discovers the New World. As Spanish settlements are established in the Americas during the next few years, the need for manpower skyrockets.

1565   The Spanish introduce slavery in North America. They take slaves to St. Augustine, the first permanent settlement in what would become Florida.

1619   A Dutch vessel arrives in Jamestown (Virginia), an English colony, with twenty slaves. These are the first slaves in an English colony in America.

1641   The colony of Massachusetts forbids slavery except in the case of war captives or people willingly selling themselves into slavery.

1652   The colony of Rhode Island is the first to forbid all forms of slavery.

1701   The War of Spanish Succession greatly weakens Spain and Portugal. England now becomes the main supplier of slaves.

1787   The Society for the Abolition of the Slave Trade is founded in England. A small colony is established in Sierra Leone, Africa, for former slaves.

1807   England outlaws the importation of slaves.

1808   The United States outlaws the importation of slaves.

1822   Liberia is founded as an African colony for freed American slaves.

1833   England outlaws slavery in all British colonies and in England itself. The American Anti-Slavery Society is formed. Arthur Tappan launches the abolitionist newspaper, the *Emancipator*. Prudence Crandall accepts black students in her school.

1836 The gag rule, which prohibits the reading of antislavery petitions in the U.S. Congress, is passed.

1837 Abolitionist Elijah Lovejoy is murdered on November 7.

1839 Cinque is captured and taken to Cuba. He leads a revolt aboard the *Amistad* on July 1. He and the other mutineers are captured on August 26 near Long Island (New York) and are brought to Connecticut. An investigative hearing is held on August 29. The *Amistad* blacks are charged with murder and piracy. In September, Cinque and the others appear in circuit court in New Haven.

1840 In January, *Amistad* Africans appear in district court. The Liberty Party, established by abolitionists, has a candidate in the presidential election.

1841 On February 20, the *Amistad* case reaches the U.S. Supreme Court. A verdict is announced on March 9. Cinque and the others leave for Africa in November.

1846 Two-year war with Mexico begins, which results in territorial gains for the U.S. in the West.

1850 The Compromise of 1850 attempts to keep a balance of power between free and slaveholding states in the U.S. Congress. Neither side is happy.

1852 Publication of *Uncle Tom's Cabin*, a novel about slavery by Harriet Beecher Stowe.

1859 John Brown leads a group of abolitionists in a raid on

Harpers Ferry, Virginia, to get weapons for an all-out slave revolt.

1861   The Civil War begins. One of the major causes of the conflict is the issue of slavery.

1863   President Abraham Lincoln issues the Emancipation Proclamation. This frees all slaves in Confederate states that the Union Army occupies and keeps England from giving further support to the South for the rest of the war. England now sees the war as one to end slavery.

1865   The Thirteenth Amendment to the U.S. Constitution is passed. It outlaws slavery in America.

1.

Captured!

UNAWARE THAT HIS LIFE would forever be changed in only a matter of minutes, twenty-five-year-old Cinque (Seen-kay) was enjoying a quiet walk in his African homeland in early 1839. This land, known as Mende country, was part of Sierra Leone, which is located on the west coast of Africa. Cinque paused now and then as he strolled down the long road to look at the lush countryside that he loved, and he studied the nearby rice fields, one of which he intended to plant soon. He smiled when he looked at his plot of rich land. The future, he thought, was most promising.

But just ahead four Africans who had been looking for Cinque hid themselves in the bushes, and when he was within reach, they jumped him. Although Cinque was strong, he was no match for four men who had the element of surprise on their side. He was quickly bound and then given a choice of marching before his attackers or being dragged on the dirt road behind them. He agreed to walk.

At first Cinque, who could get few answers from his attackers, believed that his capture was a terrible mistake. But later he remembered the fact that he had been unable to pay off a debt on time. Well aware that money lenders in West Africa sometimes sold slow-paying debtors to the slave market to recover their loans, he now suspected that he had been kidnapped to be sold.

Cinque knew that if his suspicion was correct, his future and the futures of his wife and three young children were in terrible jeopardy. Believing that he would never again see his family, he felt a deepening sorrow that was greater than he ever thought possible. At the same time, he was overwhelmed with worry for his loved ones. Were they safe, he wondered over and over, or had they, too, been captured?

Cinque's fear that he was about to become a slave was confirmed when he and his captors reached the village of Genduma, where the kidnappers sold him to Bamadzha, the son of King Shark. Before being purchased, Cinque was forced to endure a typical physical examination for slaves. He was stripped and thoroughly searched for any weakness or sign of disease. He was also poked and prodded and told to jump up and down so that his strength and endurance might be judged. When every inch of his body had been studied, he endured yet

THIS PORTRAIT OF CINQUE by Nathaniel Jocelyn was completed in late 1839 or early 1840. Courtesy of the New Haven Colony Historical Society.

another humiliation: listening to his captors and would-be buyer argue about how much he was worth.

About one month later, Bamadzha decided to sell Cinque and several other slaves. The prince took them to Lomboko, an island off the west coast that was controlled by a notorious slave dealer, a Spaniard named Pedro Blanco.

Lomboko

European slave traders began to claim certain areas along the west coast of Africa in the early 1500s. They did so both to protect a particular country's slave-trading interests in the area—many European nations engaged in the trade—as well as to provide a spot where slaves could be held until the next ship arrived to take them away. To hold on to their claims, traders built forts. These sites were heavily manned by gun-toting guards to prevent slaves from escaping and to fend off raids from other traders.

Pedro Blanco's fort, one of the largest and most successful in the area, contained a number of watchtowers and buildings. His complex also included a comfortable house with broad porches, or verandas, where traders held lengthy negotiations for the slaves. Sometimes Blanco stayed here, even though he had a mansion not too far away. Blanco's fort also had a large storehouse, several round huts with thatched roofs to house Blanco's employees, and large barracoons (barracks) for the slaves.

Unlike the typical stone barracoons found in other forts, Blanco's slave quarters were tall log fortresses. Usually slaves were not chained when they were inside the barracoons, but this varied, depending upon how rebellious the slaves appeared to be when brought into Lomboko. Cinque remained in Blanco's barracoon for almost two months.

During this time, the captives were allowed to talk to each other, although communication was sometimes difficult. Many prisoners spoke different languages and dialects, which made it impossible for them to understand each other. However, due to the sheer number of slaves being held at any one time—at least two or three hundred—a captive could usually find someone who spoke a common language. The slaves exchanged stories of their captures, of their families back home, and what they thought was going to happen to them since they seldom learned much from their captors or guards. And as the captives shared stories and made impossible escape plans, they also learned a great deal about slavery.

Most of the captives knew that slavery existed, for many people and numerous nationalities, including Africans, had engaged in the practice since ancient times. The first West African slaves taken by Europeans were captured in 1441 by the Portuguese when they explored Sierra Leone and the surrounding area. Although these slaves created great curiosity when they arrived in Europe, as had other slaves before them, at that time the Europeans had no need for a large slave population.

The demand for slaves skyrocketed, however, after the discovery of the New World in the late 1400s. Spanish colonists in the West Indies, and later colonists in what was to become the southern United States, wanted a strong, cheap labor force. They needed workers who were accustomed to working in heat and high humidity to toil in their sugar cane, rice, and cotton fields. From then on, almost any young African from the tropics was fair game for enslavement, and most of Cinque's fellow captives probably knew someone who had been taken to Lomboko.

As Cinque talked to the others, he learned that not all the prisoners had been taken because they had been tardy in paying off a debt. Some were enslaved for breaking tribal laws. Others had been taken in terrifying slave raids led by greedy men, both African and European. During these raids, men, women, and children were forced out of their homes when their villages were set on fire and then captured as they tried to flee the flames. The rest had been taken as prisoners of war during the many battles that raged between different tribes. Hatred between the tribes was so strong—and the fees for slaves were so high—that the tribes were never willing to band together to put an end to the slave trade. Many actually welcomed the practice, seeing slavery as a way to get rid of enemies and make a profit at the same time.

No matter what the reason was for enslaving someone or how it was done, the numbers mounted over the years, creating some shocking statistics. Although many historians believe

CAPTIVES WERE CHAINED TOGETHER before being marched to the coast of Africa, where they were sold. Courtesy of the Library of Congress.

that about 10 million slaves were taken from western Africa and sent to the New World, others estimate that as many as 20 to 40 million[1] were enslaved between the late 1400s and early 1800s.

The Middle Passage

The international slave trade involved a three-part journey that formed a triangle on a map. A slaver set sail from either the

American colonies, later the United States, or Europe. His ship, loaded with rum and fabrics, sailed to forts in Africa, such as Lomboko. Here the ship's captain sold the goods to fort owners, who would exchange these products for new captives brought into the barracoons in the coming months.

After a ship's initial cargo had been unloaded at the fort, slaves were taken on board for the second leg of the triangle, or the middle passage, a voyage from Africa to the West Indies or America. Upon arrival, the slaves were sold, and some of the huge profits from their sale were used to buy large quantities of the raw materials, such as sugar and cotton, that slave labor produced in these places.

These products were then loaded onto the slave ship and taken on the third leg of the voyage to the vessel's final destination, its home port in Europe or America. Here eager merchants purchased the sugar and cotton from the ship. These raw materials were turned into rum and fabric, which were then sold to slavers for more triangular voyages. This trade continued for more than two hundred years, and many merchants became very wealthy because of slavery without ever seeing or owning a slave.

When the captives had been lined up in the barracoons in preparation for boarding a ship for the middle passage, the fort's owner and his guards brought the prisoners out for inspection. The ship's captain and doctor both examined the slaves for any sign of disease. John Barbot, a slave trader, described a typical scene:

[The slaves] are brought out into a large plain, where the surgeons examine every part of every one of them to the smallest member, men and women being all stark naked. [Those found] good and sound are set on one side. . . . Each [who has] passed . . . is marked on the breast with a red-hot iron, imprinting the mark of the . . . companies.[2]

In April when Cinque boarded the slave ship *Tecora*, a Portuguese vessel, he was one of five hundred Africans to do so. This ship was well equipped for its middle passage. The deck was like a prison, surrounded with barricades and high nets held in place with stout poles. These barriers were supposed to prevent slaves from committing suicide by jumping overboard and drowning themselves as some had done in the past when they realized that they were about to leave Africa forever.

Once aboard the *Tecora*, the slaves were divided. Women and children were assigned to a separate area; they were not put in chains because they were not considered a threat to the crew's safety. The men, however, were regarded with great fear because they outnumbered crew members and were strong. Therefore, male slaves were heavily restrained. Each man's hands and feet were chained together. In addition, every man was forced to wear a heavy iron collar so that the captain could chain a number of slaves together by their necks to further hobble them if he wished.

Once the men were in irons, they were taken to one of

several lower decks in the hold of the ship. Each deck in the *Tecora* had about four feet of space from floor to ceiling, which in slave ships was unusually high. Most had less than three feet between such decks so that as many layers of slaves as possible could be transported on each voyage. The men had to bend down in order to enter the area. More and more slaves were crammed in. They were forced to lie on the floor with no space between them and without even a blanket to cover themselves. For almost two months of a rough voyage, the men lay all day and night in the dark depths of the ship except for meals.

The hold was hot and poorly ventilated. The men perspired heavily, and body odors built up quickly. In addition, the crude toilet facilities—open tubs—were very difficult to reach in the crowded hold, so most men relieved themselves where they lay. The strench that resulted was almost unbearable.

Once the ship was far from the coast, the threat of revolt was less because the slaves couldn't sail the vessel themselves. The men were then taken to the upper deck to eat and get some fresh air while their quarters were cleaned with water and vinegar. Even though a mutiny was less likely than before, nervous crew members took special precautions. The mealtime that Captain Thomas Phillips described aboard his ship would have varied little on other slave vessels:

[The slaves] are fed twice a day, at 10 in the morning, and 4 in the evening, which is the time they are aptest to

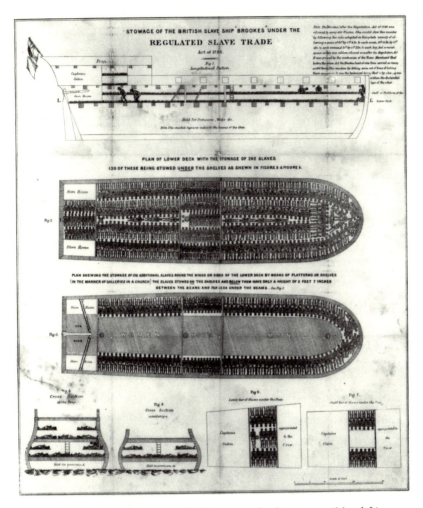

SLAVE SHIPS WERE DESIGNED to hold as many bodies as possible. African captives were crammed into each deck, where they lay, side by side, with very little space between or above them. Slaves barely had enough room to sit up during the voyage. Note the sitting slaves in the top of this illustration. Courtesy of the Library of Congress.

mutiny, being all upon deck; [the crewmen] not employ'd in distributing [food] stand to their arms; some with lighted matches at the great guns. . . . When [the slaves] have eaten their victuals clean up (which we force them to . . .), they are order'd down between decks, and every one as he passes [gets] a pint of water.[3]

Because some slaves attempted to commit suicide at sea by refusing to eat, the *Tecora*'s crew watched for any sign that captives were trying to starve themselves to death. The first slave caught doing so was publicly punished in order to scare the others into being more cooperative. Such slaves were whipped until they either agreed to eat again or they died from the beating.

Slaves also died from disease. The enormous stress that the blacks were under weakened their immune systems, as did the poor diet and lack of exercise. In addition, the unsanitary conditions aboard the vessels allowed bacteria to thrive, and contagious diseases spread rapidly in the confined quarters. Cholera, which causes severe diarrhea and vomiting, was only one of many common diseases aboard slavers. Because medications such as antibiotics did not exist, crew members took drastic action at the first sign of sickness to protect their profits. Ailing slaves were unchained and tossed overboard. More than one-third of those who boarded the vessel at Lomboko died at sea from one cause or another.

Land at Last

In early June, a few days before the *Tecora* reached Havana, Cuba, its destination in the Spanish West Indies, the treatment of the slaves improved greatly. This was not due to any humanitarian feelings on the part of the crew; it was simply a good business practice to try to present the surviving slaves in as good a condition as possible to potential buyers. As a result, Cinque and the others were brought on deck for longer periods of time, where they were exercised and bathed. They were also given clothing as well as larger portions of food and water. Even so, the slaves were no less fearful of the crew than they had been before.

The slaves' fears increased when they neared Cuba. Instead of entering the harbor, the ship suddenly stopped and waited for nightfall. Meanwhile, it seemed as if every crew member was scanning the horizon, looking for trouble. The slaves sensed the apprehension of the crew, but they had no way of knowing that the slavers were on the lookout for patrol ships, especially those manned by the British. If a patrol ship's captain spotted the *Tecora*, his crew could board the vessel and free the slaves. The crew could also take enough evidence to make sure that the *Tecora*'s sailors were hanged. Transporting slaves from Africa was an illegal act in 1839, punishable by death.

That night, frightened slaves were taken to shore and

hidden in a warehouse located approximately three miles from the coast. About one week later, the prisoners were marched to Havana, giving the impression, the slavers hoped, that these slaves were not new to the island but had been purchased from inland plantations.

Once the captives arrived in Havana, they were put into huge roofless pens in the center of town. Local citizens stopped by to inspect the newest arrivals, and the pens were a tourist site as well. Townspeople often took their guests downtown to see the slaves. Among those examining the *Tecora*'s prisoners were two Spaniards, Jose Ruiz and Pedro Montes, experienced slave owners.

Ten days later, Ruiz bought forty-nine men, including Cinque, and Montes purchased four children, three girls and a boy. The buyers planned to take these Africans to Puerto Príncipe, Cuba. Their plans, however, were dramatically changed by Cinque.

2.

Mutiny on the *Amistad*

SHORTLY AFTER MAKING their purchases, Jose Ruiz and Pedro Montes chartered a Spanish ship, the *Amistad,* to transport the slaves. This vessel also carried many boxes of manufactured goods, which Ruiz valued at $40,000, a lot of money in those days. The *Amistad* (ironically, the Spanish word for "friendship"), was owned and commanded by Captain Ramon Ferrer. He was accompanied by two slaves—a cabin boy, Antonio, and a cook named Celestino—and two crew members. The *Amistad* set sail for Puerto Príncipe, Cuba, on June 28, 1839.

Strangely enough, even though the crew was vastly outnumbered, seven sailors to fifty-three slaves, none of the forty-nine African men were chained during the day. Instead, all of the captives were allowed to move about the hold at will, and once the ship was at sea, a few at a time were even allowed up on deck.

Although the voyage was normally no more than three days long, the weather proved to be uncooperative. The winds died down, and the vessel sat still in the water beneath a blazing hot sun for hours on end, with sails slack. Not knowing how long the journey might take now, the crew decided to ration both food and water. Each slave was to receive only one banana, two potatoes, and half a cup of water each day.

The lack of food and water and the intense heat made the slaves edgy and extremely uncomfortable. When one of them tried to take more than his daily allowance of water to ease his thirst, a crew member responded quickly, giving the captive a sound thrashing. This beating was hardly the first aboard the ship; the captain often used the lash to instill fear in the slaves.

Determining the Future

While the ship sat still, Cinque decided to find out what was going to happen to him and the others. He approached Celestino first. The cook thought that it would be amusing to torment Cinque, so he made up a ghastly story. With a big smile on his face, the cook used sign language and pointed to lots of pots and knives to indicate that Cinque and the others were soon going to be slaughtered, cut up, salted down, and eaten.

Although this sickened Cinque, it did not surprise him. After all he had seen and endured since being captured, he knew that white men were savages who were capable of great crimes and atrocities. What made this situation especially horrible, however, was the fact that the Africans would be eaten by the likes of Captain Ferrer. Such a revolting fate was more than Cinque could accept, and so he began to plan a mutiny.

Fortunately for Cinque, he had chosen the perfect time to start an uprising. This was true for at least four reasons. First, the slaves' greater freedom during the day allowed them to find the tools they needed to free themselves from their chains at night, the best time to catch the crew off guard. Second, most of the forty-nine men were Mendes. Not only did they speak the same language, which made plotting easy, they were also used to working together for the common good. All young men in Mende country became members of a "poro," a group in which they were expected to discuss problems and find solutions. Third, the slaves were willing to risk a revolt because they thought it was the only way to remain alive. And fourth, the *Amistad* crew was careless.

Cinque was assisted in his scheming by Burnah and Grabeau (Grab-oh). Burnah, the captive who tried to take an extra drink of water, was resourceful and strong. He had been a blacksmith in his Mende homeland. Grabeau was a Mende from the village of Fulu. Like Cinque, he was a husband, a father, and a rice planter. Grabeau was about five feet tall, quick and daring, and he spoke three African dialects.

GRABEAU, SECOND IN COMMAND during the *Amistad* mutiny, convinced Cinque to spare the lives of Ruiz and Montes, believing that they could sail the captives back to Africa. Portrait by William H. Townsend, 1839. Courtesy of Beinecke Rare Book and Manuscript Library, Yale University.

To Arms!

As the slaves milled about the deck, they looked for anything that might help them. Cinque eventually found a nail that could be used to pick the lock on his shackles while the crew slept.

On the night of June 30, shortly after the slaves had been chained, Cinque freed himself. Once he had mastered the technique, he released the rest of the men.

Then, as planned, the slaves began to search the ship for weapons. They started by prying open a number of boxes in the hold meant for delivery in Puerto Príncipe. Eventually, they opened a crate that contained machetes. These knives, which were used to cut down sugar cane, had deadly sharp blades that were two feet long.

The actual attack started around 4 A.M. on July 1. Cinque led the men onto the upper deck, where they discovered Captain Ferrer, who often slept in the open when the weather was especially warm. Unlike the captain's cabin, the deck afforded Ferrer no protection. He barely had time to call out for help before Cinque and the others were upon him. Ferrer killed one African and wounded two others in the struggle, but he couldn't hold off the attack, even though Ruiz and Montes came to his aid. Seizing an opportunity to finish off the captain, Cinque swung his machete hard enough to knock Ferrer to the deck. But before Cinque could actually kill the captain,

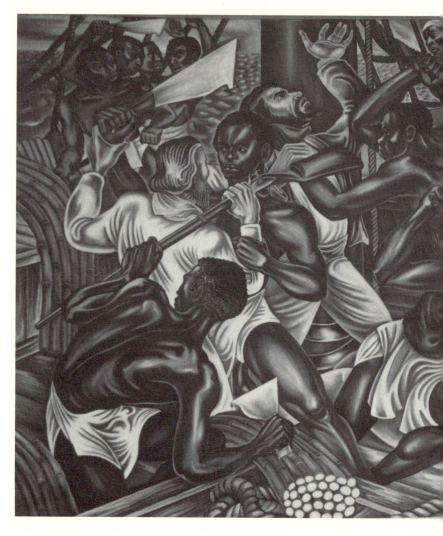

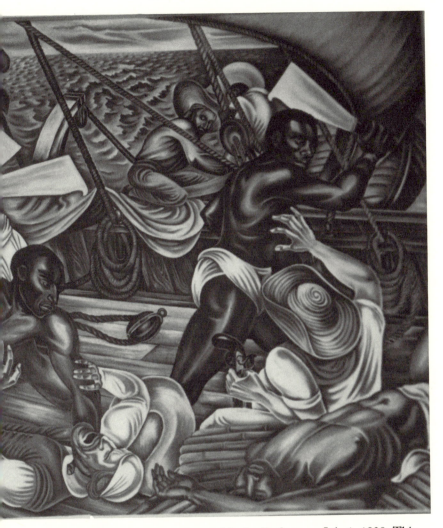

THE AFRICANS STRUCK QUICKLY with deadly force on July 1, 1839. This version of the revolt was painted by Hale Woodruff in 1939. Note the crewmen abandoning the ship in the background. This painting is part of a mural about the *Amistad* captives on display at Talladega College in Talladega, Alabama. Courtesy of Talladega College.

other Africans fell upon him, strangling him to death with their bare hands.

While Cinque was attacking Ferrer, a small group hunted down the hated cook. When they found him, they hacked him to death with their knives. Their rage was so great that they continued to slash and stab Celestino long after he was dead.

Ruiz and Montes realized that they were in a dangerous position as soon as they reached the deck and saw the armed Africans; even so, they did their best to end the revolt. But with the loss of the captain and the cook, they were in an impossible position. The young cabin boy Antonio was too small to be of any help, and the two crewmen were nowhere to be seen. They had abandoned the ship at the first sign of trouble, getting away in a small boat. Ruiz decided to surrender when the Africans charged at him. Montes tried, unsuccessfully, to hide below deck after being seriously wounded.

Now Cinque, Burnah, and Grabeau were in charge of the *Amistad,* and all of the captives, including the four children who witnessed the mutiny, were filled with relief. None, though, was foolish enough to think that all their troubles were over.

Going Home

The Africans wanted nothing more than to go home, but none of them had ever sailed a ship. Cinque had noticed that while they were on the voyage from Africa they sailed into a setting sun each day. He reasoned that if the ship sailed toward a rising sun, they could eventually reach Sierra Leone. Ruiz and Montes were then told to sail the ship to Africa or die.

From the beginning, the Spaniards decided not to cooperate. Both men believed that their only hope of staying alive was to sail to the eastern coast of the United States, where American authorities might spot them, seize the ship, and free them. So during the day, whoever was in charge set the *Amistad*'s course for the east and the rising sun but rigged the ship's sails so that they caught as little wind as possible. At night, without the sun to give them away, Ruiz and Montes changed the ship's course, steering the vessel west and north and turning the sails so that the ship could make speedy progress. As a result of the Spaniards' efforts, the *Amistad* made a most unusual voyage, zigzagging across the water and up the eastern coast of the United States.

More than once, Cinque suspected that the ship was not headed to Africa, and he repeatedly threatened the Spaniards with death. Ruiz and Montes responded by begging for their lives, assuring Cinque that they were following orders. Each time such an incident occurred, though, the Spaniards had to wonder how much longer they could deceive Cinque.

Living conditions on the ship became unbearable when the available water and foodstuffs had to be rationed. Some Africans became so desperate for something to drink that they sampled the liquids that they found on the vessel, including bottles of medicine. Several died as a result. The shortages of food and water, the death of comrades aboard the ship (ten had died since boarding the *Amistad*), and the nagging suspicion that Ruiz and Montes were not taking them home to Sierra Leone filled many with despair.

While the *Amistad* meandered across the water, some ships spotted the vessel, and several even approached her to see if she was in distress. The Africans managed to communicate their need for food and water, and they were able to secure both from at least one captain, purchasing the goods with some of the gold coins they found on the vessel. To keep their revolt a secret, the Africans hid Ruiz and Montes below deck whenever another ship was nearby, and they limited the number of visitors who might board the *Amistad* at one time to a handful.

It's unlikely that many sailors wanted to go aboard, though, at least not without being heavily armed. The *Amistad* had become a strange looking wreck of a ship. It flew no flag, its mast was broken, and its sails were ragged and torn. All were signs of an incompetent or inexperienced crew.

And then there was the frightening appearance of the *Amistad*'s sailors. Few crews aboard Spanish ships consisted entirely of Africans at that time, and even fewer waved machetes about. In addition, typical crewmen never wore anything that resembled the costumes seen on the *Amistad*. Some of the slaves had abandoned the clothing that they had been given on the *Tecora*, draping themselves instead with fabric that they found in the ship's hold—silks, satins, and colorful cottons—or putting together unusual outfits from boxes of clothing. Cinque, for example, wore a red flannel shirt and white pantaloons.

As more and more sailors spotted the *Amistad* and described her when they reached shore, people all along America's eastern seaboard began to look for the strange vessel. And when they saw it, or thought that they did, their imaginations ran wild. Some said that the *Amistad* was clearly a pirate ship with swashbuckling black buccaneers. Others insisted that it was the *Flying Dutchman,* a ghost ship full of sinners that according to legend, was destined to sail until the world ended. And a handful thought—feared!—that it was a vessel whose crew was ravaged by a deadly tropical disease, a crew desperately looking for a port.

A newspaper article that appeared in the Columbia, South Carolina *Columbian Centinel* on August 23 mentioned gold doubloons, or coins, on board, and this piqued the public's curiosity even more. This article described Captain Sears's encounter with the *Amistad* near the New England coast:

> Sears . . . fell in with a . . . schooner of about eighty tons, with a crew of blacks, about thirty in number, and from their signs understood they wanted water. Upon boarding her, he found the sails in bad order, umbrellas, looking-glasses, crockery, etc., strewn about the decks, and understood they had been out about three months, that the captain was sick and all the white people had been

washed overboard. The crew were armed with knives, and doubloons were plenty among them, one of which Captain Sears received for some provisions.[4]

Long Island, New York

The *Amistad* had been spotted frequently off the eastern coast in mid-August, and by late August the vessel had arrived at Culloden Point on the eastern end of Long Island, New York. Desperate for food and water, Cinque decided to drop anchor here and go into a nearby port to try to buy supplies.

On August 25, Cinque, Burnah, Grabeau, and five other men took a small boat and rowed toward land. Upon arriving, the men went from house to house to try to buy food, and although they had little success in getting supplies simply because no one understood what they wanted, they were very successful in drawing attention to themselves.

When the Africans returned to their small boat, they were approached by Captain Henry Green and several of his friends, who had entered the port earlier and had spotted the blacks on the beach. Green was most interested in Cinque and the *Amistad,* believing that it might be the mysterious ship he had heard about, and if so, it might be loaded with pirate loot. Green had dreams of luring everyone ashore and then claiming the ship for himself. For his part, Cinque was interested in the seamen because he thought that they could get the *Amistad*

THIS ILLUSTRATION, by an unknown artist, shows some of the *Amistad* captives bargaining for water and supplies with inhabitants of Long Island, N.Y. In the background lies the *Amistad* with its tattered sails. Courtesy of the New Haven Colony Historical Society.

back to Africa. The men talked for a while, using hand gestures to try to get their story across.

The following day Cinque and several others met Green on the beach again. They were trying to communicate when the USS *Washington,* an American patrol vessel, suddenly appeared. Under the orders of Lt. Commander T.R. Gedney, who felt strongly that something about the *Amistad* was amiss, the crew of the *Washington* seized the *Amistad,* its cargo, and its crew for examination.

Cinque alerted his comrades on the beach when he saw the *Washington* approaching the *Amistad.* The panic-stricken Africans then rowed as fast as possible toward the *Amistad* to warn the others and encourage them to resist, believing that they would be enslaved again. These men were forced back to the beach by several American sailors in small boats. After a desperate attempt to hide on shore, the Africans were captured. All were taken to the *Amistad* under guard.

The Africans still on board the *Amistad* were overjoyed to see Cinque again. He spoke to them at length, and as he did so, the Africans' mood changed. The blacks became restless and angry. The Americans, believing correctly that Cinque was suggesting another mutiny, decided to isolate him on the *Washington.*

Gedney wanted to claim the ship and its contents, including the Africans, who, he was reasonably sure, were escaped slaves. He had two choices: He could take his prize to New York, which had outlawed slavery, or he could take the *Amistad* to Connecticut, just north of Long Island, where slavery, although being phased out, was still legal. Since Gedney would most likely find greater support for his claims in Connecticut, he decided to go there. The *Amistad* was towed to New London on August 27.

Gedney knew that claiming his prize would mean going through the court system, and he was eager to have his claim heard. The same day he arrived, he notified the federal district judge of Connecticut, Andrew T. Judson, about the *Amistad,* asking for a hearing as soon as possible.

Until Judson arrived, all of the Africans, except Cinque, were held aboard the *Amistad.* As they waited, they worried once again about what their futures held. These frightened men and terrorized children had no way of knowing how difficult the days ahead would be; nor could they possibly have imagined that they were about to become part of a court case that would make history in the United States.

3.

Judson Holds a Hearing

WHILE MANY CURIOSITY SEEKERS waited to learn the outcome, Judge Andrew Judson held an investigative hearing aboard the *Washington* on August 29, two days after he had been notified that the *Amistad* was in New London's harbor. Although Lt. Commander Gedney had hoped to file his claim and get a quick decision, nothing was to go as fast as Gedney wanted. First, Judson had to determine exactly what had happened on the *Amistad*.

The judge began the hearing by examining the *Amistad*'s papers. These papers included passports for the crew and slave traders, trading licenses, lists of the cargo carried aboard the vessel, and official papers from the customs house. All appeared to be in order, and on the surface, they seemed to prove that the *Amistad* was a legitimate trading vessel owned by a

Spanish subject, Captain Ferrer, who was operating within the law.

Next, the passports for the captives were examined. Several clues indicated that these papers were not accurate. For example, none of the Africans answered to any of the names Judson read from the papers, names such as Manuel, Philip, and Augustine. It isn't surprising that the captives didn't recognize their new Spanish names since they had never used them before. The new names were another ploy, like marching the captives overland in Cuba, to convince authorities, if the situation required it, that the Africans were "ladinos," slaves who had been living in Cuba for a long time.

Another clue was the fact that none of the Africans could speak or understand any Spanish. Spain had reluctantly agreed to stop importing slaves in 1817 when it was pressured to do so by Great Britain. This agreement went into effect in 1820. Therefore, if the passports were correct, the slaves on the *Amistad* in 1839 had either lived in Cuba for the past nineteen years, which was more than enough time to learn some Spanish, or they had been born on the island. Despite these problems, Judson failed to question the passports for reasons that are not clear.

Eyewitnesses

After Judge Judson was finished looking at the papers, he listened to testimony from Ruiz, Montes, and Antonio. Lt.

Commander Gedney, who spoke Spanish, served as an interpreter. None of the Africans could testify because none could speak any language that the court could understand.

Ruiz testified first. He began by describing the mutiny:

> For the first four days everything went on well. In the night heard a noise in the forecastle [of the ship]. All of us were asleep except the man at the helm. Do not know how things began; was [awakened] by the noise. This man Joseph [Cinque's Spanish name] I saw. Cannot tell how many were engaged. There was no moon. It was very dark. I took up an oar and tried to quell the mutiny; I cried no! no! I then heard one of the crew cry murder. . . . I went below and called on Montes to follow me. . . . I did not see the captain killed. . . . The slaves told us next day that they had killed all; but the cabin boy said they had killed only the captain and cook.[5]

Montes was the next to testify. After giving details of the mutiny that supported Ruiz's version, he described the repeated threats on his life afterward.

> Every moment my life was threatened. . . . The prisoners treated me harshly, and but for the interference of [Grabeau, Cinque] would have killed me several times every day. . . . I had no wish to kill any of them, but prevented them from killing each other.[6]

Exactly how Montes kept the Africans from killing each other was never explained. The statement, however, made him seem kind.

The court then adjourned to the *Amistad* so that the judge might see firsthand where the mutiny took place. It was here that Antonio, the cabin boy, described the revolt, and it was here that he specifically identified the leaders of the mutiny.

The witnesses had given damning evidence against the captives. All three described a peaceful scene aboard a shipload of slaves until the mutiny occurred, and all claimed that they either saw the Africans attack and kill the captain and cook or heard the men confess to the dastardly act afterward. The repeated threats against Montes did little to help the Africans' cause, and the fact that Antonio could actually identify the leaders cinched the case against Cinque, Burnah, and Grabeau. The Africans were regarded as slaves who had forgotten their place—slaves were forbidden to revolt—and they were charged with murder as well as piracy for taking the ship. Both crimes were punishable by death.

Prisoners Again

The Africans, including the children, were then taken to a jail in nearby New Haven, Connecticut, where they were to be held until mid-September, when a trial was scheduled. The children were to serve as eyewitnesses, if an interpreter could be found. Although the Africans could not understand the case against them, they understood enough of what went on to know that they were in serious trouble. Once again, they were overcome with despair.

4.

Abolitionists to the Rescue

WHEN JUDGE JUDSON HELD his investigation on the USS *Washington*, he allowed newspaper reporters and several interested spectators to attend the hearing. Among the spectators was Dwight P. Janes, an abolitionist, who, like all abolitionists, wanted to end slavery in the United States immediately.

The idea of freeing the slaves in America was not new. In fact, the issue of slavery was a hotly debated topic when the Constitutional Convention met in 1787 to set up a new government. How, antislavery delegates demanded, could Americans fight in a revolution for freedom and then deny freedom to others? Southern delegates insisted upon protecting their property, including slaves, and these delegates made it perfectly clear that they would not support any constitution that made slavery illegal. In order to hold the delegates—and the country—together, the Convention sidestepped the issue by turning it back to the states, allowing them to decide for themselves whether or not to permit slavery within their borders. The issue of slavery was not settled, though, and less than one hundred years later, it became one of the causes of the Civil War (1861–1865), the results of which are still being felt today.

Although the number of abolitionists in the 1700s was small, members were very active, and they were able to find some supporters. But it wasn't until the 1820s that the abolitionist movement began to gather steam. At that time, the spirit of change swept over America. Public-minded reformers tried to make the United States a better place for all, and they developed an impressive program. They wanted more educational opportunities for young people, more rights for women, better treatment for the mentally ill, more help for the poor, and an end to war.

At the same time, a religious revival swept over the country, especially among Christians. More people attended church than ever before, and day-long worship services drew people from near and far. Church leaders urged the faithful to reform America by fighting sin with all their might to create a great Christian nation that would truly please God.

Abolitionists used the spirit of reform and religious zeal of the day to further their cause. They argued that slavery, besides being a sin, was one of the sources of hatred and violence in American society. Therefore, until slavery was abolished, society could never really be improved, let alone pleasing in God's sight. Abolitionists then asked for the support of all reformers.

In the early 1830s, the number of abolitionists grew slowly but steadily. By 1831, the American Colonization Society had raised enough money to purchase almost 1,500 slaves and send them back to Africa to live in colonies in Liberia and Sierra Leone. A national society, the American Anti-Slavery Society, was formed in 1833. And William Lloyd Garrison, one of America's most famous abolitionists, began to write a newspaper in 1833, the *Liberator,* to convince others to join his cause.

To gain even more supporters, abolitionists produced many pamphlets, gave lectures, and petitioned Congress to abolish slavery. These actions attracted more members, but the number of abolitionists was not large, probably never more than 200,000.

Fighting the Abolitionists

Although a growing number of Americans disliked slavery by 1830, most of them thought that the slave issue might resolve itself over time. Many believed that since the importation of slaves had been outlawed, slavery would simply die out. This belief was not realistic, however, because the number of slaves

WILLIAM LLOYD GARRISON (1805–1879), an avid abolitionist, founded *The Liberator,* an abolitionist newspaper. His first edition contained the now-famous words about his dedication to freeing the slaves. He wrote, "I am in earnest—I will not equivocate—I will not excuse—I will not retreat a single inch—and *I will be heard.*" Garrison's determination frightened and upset the public. Courtesy of the Library of Congress.

LEWIS TAPPAN (1788–1873) was a wealthy merchant and a dedicated abolitionist. He used a large portion of his fortune to finance various causes to help free the slaves. Engraving by Philip H. Reason. Courtesy of the Dover Pictorial Archives.

MARTIN VAN BUREN
(1782–1862) had a long
political life. He was U.S.
Senator from New York,
governor of that state,
President Andrew Jackson's
secretary of state, and Jackson's
vice president, before being
elected president in 1836. He
was plagued by the slavery issue
throughout his term as the
abolitionists gained strength
and demanded to be heard.
Portrait by Eliphalet Fraser
Andrews. Courtesy of the
Dover Pictorial Archives.

ROGER SHERMAN BALDWIN
(1793–1863) was deeply
opposed to slavery. He was the
grandson of Roger Sherman,
who signed both the
Declaration of Independence
and the U.S. Constitution.
Baldwin was first a lawyer and
then a politician, representing
Connecticut in the U.S. Senate
from 1847 to 1851. He also
served as the state's governor.
Engraving by Alexander H.
Ritchie. Courtesy of the Dover
Pictorial Archives.

continued to increase at a steady rate due to a rising birth rate among blacks. In 1820 there were 1.5 million slaves in the United States; in 1860, just before the Civil War began, there were almost 4 million.

In addition to believing that the problem would go away and therefore could be ignored, many Americans were deeply opposed to immediate freedom for the slaves for at least three reasons. First, the labor that slaves provided was important to the entire American economy. For example, the cotton that slaves produced not only made money for plantation owners, it was the major fiber used in Northern textile mills. Besides being vital to the nation's economy, slave labor would be difficult to replace. If the slaves were set free, few blacks would be willing to continue toiling from dawn to dusk in the fields, and there were not enough unemployed workers in the South to take their places. A labor shortage would mean that fewer crops could be produced, and both the Northern and Southern economies would suffer.

Second, slave labor was free. Even if workers were available, plantation owners would have to pay them wages, which would cut into the enormous profits they were enjoying. This would mean that the price of cotton would go up and that the textile mills would have to raise the price of the cloth they sold. Many Northerners were also afraid that if the slaves were freed, they would head north and take jobs away from white workers because the former slaves would be willing to work for lower wages.

Americans also resisted freeing the slaves because of racial prejudice. For years, Americans, and especially slaveowners, had convinced themselves that blacks were less than human in order to justify enslaving them. To support this belief, slave-holders exaggerated the physical differences between the races and insisted that blacks were mentally inferior. The proof of this claim, slaveholders argued, was that blacks came from a continent that had never produced any great civilizations. This statement wasn't accurate. The ancient Egyptians and the Kingdom of Benin in West Africa, for example, were out-standing civilizations by anyone's standards. Even so, the put-down was seldom challenged.

Also, many Americans looked down upon blacks because they weren't Christians. This was especially true when the reli-gious revival took place in the 1820s. One of the major reasons given to justify enslaving Africans was that it gave Christians a chance to convert the heathens and save their souls. In the early days of slavery, Catholic priests actually stood beside slave ships in Africa, baptizing blacks as they boarded vessels for the middle passage.

Racial prejudice was to be expected in slaveholding states. However, such prejudice was just as strong in the North. For instance, the *New York Sunday Morning News* said that blacks in the United States were "happier and better in a state of [slavery]."[7] The *Daily Express,* another New York newspaper, said that blacks were "hardly above the apes and monkeys of their own Africa."[8] And the New York *Morning Herald* insisted that God never meant for blacks and whites to live side by side "in any other relation than that of master and slave."[9]

Resistance to abolition wasn't limited to nasty comments in the newspapers. In 1836, Congress, prodded by Southern representatives, enacted a "gag rule" that prohibited anyone from introducing petitions in Congress that called for freeing the slaves. Southern postmasters fought the abolitionists by refusing to deliver their pamphlets and newsletters. And some Americans who thought that the abolitionists were nothing but troublemakers attacked antislavery leaders. William Lloyd Garrison was dragged through the streets of Boston in an attempt to scare him into abandoning his stand on slavery. The mob was not successful, though, for Garrison was so dedicated to the abolitionist cause that only death would have stopped him.

Perhaps the most famous violent incident involving an abolitionist was the murder of Elijah Lovejoy. Lovejoy was a newspaper editor in Alton, Illinois, where he published articles in favor of freeing the slaves. Shortly after his first abolitionist articles appeared, his shop was stormed by an angry mob that destroyed the paper's printing press. When friends gave Lovejoy money to buy another press, he resumed his fight to free the slaves. But on November 7, 1837, Lovejoy's shop was invaded again. This time the mob set his building on fire, and when the defiant editor vowed to continue his fight, someone in the group shot Lovejoy dead.

To Overcome Prejudice

To eliminate prejudice as a reason for not freeing the slaves, abolitionists worked to make blacks seem more like whites by educating them. These efforts raised tempers, violated laws in some states, and resulted in violence.

For example, when Prudence Crandall, a teacher in Canterbury, Connecticut, accepted blacks into her classroom, especially those from out of state, townspeople vowed to close her school. Local businesses refused to sell anything to Crandall, in the hope of forcing her to leave town. When this effort failed, townspeople insisted that a law forbidding the teaching of black students from other states in local schools be passed and then enforced. Crandall was arrested, tried, and found guilty. She appealed the decision, and while she waited for a court to overturn the decision, which it eventually did, she continued to teach. A crowd then stoned her school. Afraid for the safety of her students, Crandall reluctantly cancelled classes and left town to start another school elsewhere.

The *Amistad* Committee

Even though the abolitionists faced incredible odds, they were unwilling to give up. By the late 1830s, they were seasoned fighters, and they were constantly looking for ways to convince the public that slavery had to go. To do this, they needed some

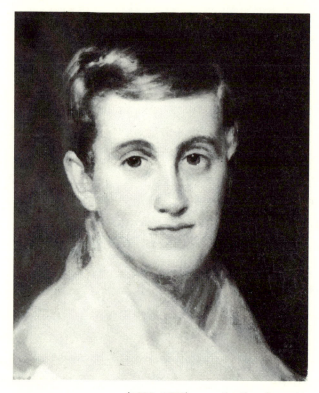

PRUDENCE CRANDALL (1803–1899) was a leading figure in the movement to educate blacks in America. She met stiff resistance from townspeople in Canterbury, Connecticut, when she admitted black students to class. Eventually, she was forced to abandon her school. Few women participated in abolitionist activities since many organizations were for men only. Besides, taking a stand on any issue in public was considered unladylike at best. Therefore, activists like Crandall were often attacked by the public and some abolitionists as well. Portrait by Francis Alexander. Courtesy of the Dover Pictorial Archives.

conflict or issue that would attract national attention as well as sympathy for slaves. When abolitionist Dwight P. Janes attended the hearing about the mutiny on the *Amistad*, he was convinced that he had found what they had been searching for.

On September 7, he met with other abolitionists in the area to form the *Amistad* Committee. This committee included Reverend Joshua Leavitt, the editor of the *Emancipator*, an abolitionist newsletter in New York City; Reverend Simeon Jocelyn, who was the minister of New Haven's first church for blacks; and Lewis Tappan, a wealthy businessman. Lewis and his brother Arthur, among the founders of the American Anti-Slavery Society, had so angered slaveholders that a reward of $100,000 was offered for the delivery of their bodies, payable in any slave state. Arthur Tappan had financed several educational projects for blacks, including Prudence Crandall's school. All of the members on the Committee knew that they might incur the wrath of Northerners and Southerners alike if they supported the captives on the *Amistad*. Neither this nor the fact that violence might result dampened their determination to take on the case.

Once the Committee was organized, the members began to lay the groundwork for the captives' defense. Leavitt agreed to comb the docks of New York's busy seaport to see if he could find some sailor who spoke the Africans' language, so that the captives could tell their side of the story. Meanwhile

Tappan and Jocelyn would begin to raise money to pay legal fees. These two men also began their search for a lawyer who would represent the Africans. The Committee never doubted that a battle royal lay ahead, for they were determined to make it so.

5.

Which Side Are You On?

WHILE JUDGE JUDSON was holding his hearing, the president of the United States, Martin Van Buren, was trying to find a noncontroversial solution to the problems that the capture of the *Amistad* presented. At first it appeared to Van Buren that he and his cabinet would be responsible for dealing with the various issues surrounding the slave ship. Van Buren, a Democrat, wanted to run for the presidency again in 1840, and he was well aware that any action on his part in the *Amistad* affair would have serious political repercussions.

On one hand, Southern Democrats, many of whom were slaveholders, would be downright angry if the captives on the *Amistad* were freed. Slaveholders believed Ruiz and Montes's story that the captives had been slaves in Cuba for many years. Southerners called the captives "assassins" and thought that they should be sent back to Cuba and hanged. Also, Southerners were afraid that if the captives were set free, other slaves would revolt in hopes of gaining their freedom. In states where slaves outnumbered whites and bloody revolts had already taken place, this was a real threat.

On the other hand, many Northern Democrats, as well as members of the public, thought that the slaves had freed themselves in the mutiny and should be allowed to go to Africa. If this didn't happen, the president would lose a lot of votes in the North.

As if this wasn't bad enough, Van Buren also faced serious international conflicts because of the capture of the *Amistad*, and this, too, threatened his re-election plans. From the beginning, Spain demanded that the *Amistad* and all its cargo and property, which, according to the Spanish government, included the slaves, should be returned to Cuba— immediately. If any trial was necessary, Spanish leaders said, they would hold it.

The Spanish foreign minister in Washington, D.C., Angel Calderón de la Barca, backed his government's demand with several rather persuasive arguments. First, the minister referred to two treaties that had been signed by the United States and Spain, the Pinckney Treaty of 1795 and the Adams-Onis Treaty of 1819. These treaties included sections that said that if any ship from one nation ended up in the other country's port due to some misfortune, the distressed ship would receive reasonable aid and be returned to its home port. The minister insisted that these sections applied to the *Amistad.* If America refused to return the ship and cargo, the minister said with great emphasis, Spain might just as well declare all sections of the treaties null and void. How, he wondered aloud, could the United States ever again be trusted to keep its promises?

Spain was eager to settle this issue as quickly as possible in order to save face and hide the truth about illegal slaves in Cuba. If the real story were told, it would look as though Spain lacked the power to enforce its own laws, or worse yet, deliberately broke treaties and then lied about it.

Also, the case increased Spain's fear of England, the country that had long led the crusade against slavery. Spain believed that if British leaders found out about the continued importation of slaves, England might intervene in Cuba, using treaties that outlawed the international slave trade as an excuse. Therefore, to keep the matter as quiet as possible, the minister insisted that the crisis should be settled between the heads of the two governments right away, not publicly in an American courtroom.

Besieged on all sides, President Van Buren turned to two members of his cabinet for advice, his secretary of state, John Forsyth, and his attorney general, Felix Grundy. Both men were slaveholders from the South, and both advised Van Buren to send the ship and captives to Cuba. These advisors argued that the terms of the treaties gave the president no other choice. Besides, the United States wanted to maintain a good relationship with Spain. Not only were there a number of Americans living in Cuba, but the United States had been eyeing the island as a possible future state. (President Polk would make the first unsuccessful offer to buy Cuba in 1848, an offer that was repeated by the next two presidents.)

But before Van Buren could act, Lt. Commander Gedney, who had captured the *Amistad,* filed an official claim in court for a reward, and Judge Judson had ordered a trial for the captives. Now there was little Van Buren could do but to step aside. If he interfered, he would be accused of overriding the courts, which would cost him votes in the North and in the South.

Building Support for the Captives

Unlike President Van Buren, the *Amistad* Committee wanted as much publicity as possible. After visiting the blacks in jail in New Haven, some Committee members wrote letters about the plight of the captives for publication in newspapers to get the public's attention.

These letters often included details about the blacks' imprisonment. At this time, all but Cinque were housed in adjoining rooms in the jail. The four children had one room to themselves, and the adult males lived in three rooms. Because Cinque was thought to be a dangerous ringleader, he was kept in another area with men who had been charged with committing violent crimes. The Africans had surrendered their color-ful costumes worn on the *Amistad*. Yards of calico and satin were replaced with dark cotton trousers and shirts. The girls were given cotton dresses and shawls, which, in true African fashion, they wore as turbans.

Although the living conditions were tolerable enough for a jail, the blacks were restless and despondent. The small win-dows in their cells provided little fresh air and only a glimpse of the outside world, and with so many bodies in each room, there was no room for exercise. In addition, the Africans still could not tell their story, and they worried constantly about what the future held, which was hardly a new situation for them. Their depression affected their appetites, and several ate very little at first. As a result, the Committee feared for the health of the prisoners.

In addition to describing the blacks' life in jail, the Com-mittee's letters to newspapers emphasized the captives' despair. The letters also hinted at the fact that the Africans might have been taken illegally from Sierra Leone.

While the Africans tried to adjust to life in jail, Commit-tee members contacted abolitionists across the country by writing about the case in national newsletters. They hoped to gain strong moral and financial support for the captives throughout the North.

These efforts were very successful, and they created great sympathy for the Africans. As a result, the captives were not only a frequent topic of the day in major newspapers and private conversations, they were the subject of a popular play as well, *The Black Schooner*. This hastily written drama appeared before large audiences in New York City only seven days after the Africans were arrested.

Artists got into the act, too. They went to the jail in New Haven, made sketches of Cinque and several others, and then sold hundreds of copies on the street, which only further increased interest in the case. Perhaps the best known portrait of Cinque was done by Nathaniel Jocelyn (see page 3), the brother of *Amistad* Committee member Simeon Jocelyn.

In a way, the Committee's efforts to make the case known were a little too successful. The campaign created so much curiosity that more than 4,000 people flocked to the jail in New Haven. Here visitors paid twelve and one-half cents apiece for a glimpse of the mysterious Africans, who were terrified at the sight of so many gawking Americans.

On Trial in Hartford

The murder and piracy trial for the Africans was scheduled for September 19, 1839, in the U.S. Circuit Court, which met in the state capitol building in Hartford, Connecticut. Because of all the publicity about the case, many spectators traveled to the city to see the captives and hear their defense. Others had come to Hartford in response to the rumors about a supposed mass hanging of blacks that had been circulating for more than a week.

Attorneys Roger Sherman Baldwin and W.S. Holabird would represent the two sides. Baldwin headed the defense team, which included two lawyers from New York, Seth Staples and Theodore Sedgwick. W.S. Holabird was a U.S. district attorney, and he would be the prosecutor in the case. Holabird was under orders from President Van Buren to get the case dismissed and moved to a courtroom in Cuba if at all possible.

In addition to criminal charges, many claims had now been filed for the ship, cargo, and captives. Besides Lt. Commander Gedney's claim of one-third of the value of the *Amistad* and its cargo as a reward for capturing the ship, Captain Green and his friends wanted a reward. They insisted that they had deliberately detained the Africans on the beach in Long Island at great risk to their lives so that Gedney could capture the *Amistad.* Ruiz and Montes wanted their slaves back, and merchants in Havana, Cuba, wanted compensation for their lost or damaged cargo. Also, Captain Ferrer's family wanted the return of the *Amistad* and Ferrer's slave, Antonio.

Because certain courts can only hear certain kinds of cases, two different courts had to be convened. The U.S. Circuit Court, led by Justice Smith Thompson of the U.S. Supreme Court, would hear the charges of murder and piracy,

Africans' Silhouettes

Like Cinque, Burnah, and Grabeau, all of the remaining male captives were indicted for murder and piracy. Ten of the forty-nine males who originally boarded the *Amistad* in Cuba died before reaching Long Island, and more died in jail before they were interviewed. The children were held as eyewitnesses.

John W. Barber was intrigued by the Africans. He visited them in jail, and once an interpreter was found, Barber interviewed each of the blacks, including the children. He took careful notes and made a silhouette of each one. Silhouettes were very popular at this time because they allowed the artist to make an exact likeness of the subject in a day and age when cameras were not common. Barber, a member of the Connecticut Historical Society, thought that the *Amistad* case was very important, and he did all he could to preserve as much information about it as possible for future generations. Here is a facsimile page of the silhouettes that were published with his *History of The Amistad Captives* in 1840. Courtesy of The New Haven Colony Historical Society.

town of Tu-ma. He was sent by his father to a village to buy clothes; on his return, he was seized by six men, and his hands tied behind; was ten days in going to Lomboko. There are high mountains in his country, rice is cultivated, people have guns; has seen elephants. *Remark.*—There is a village called Tu-ma, in the Timmani country, 60 miles from Sierra Leone, visited by Major Laing.

(7.) **Gna-kwoi** (in *Ba-lu* dialect, *second born*) was born at *Kong-go-la-hung*, the largest town in the Balu country. This town is situated on a large river called in Balu, *Za-li-ba;* and in Mendi, *Kal-wa-ra :* fish are caught in this river as large as a man's body—they are caught in nets and sometimes shot with guns. When going to the gold country to buy clothes, he was taken and sold to a Vai man who sold him to a Spaniard named *Péli.* Gna-kwoi has a wife and one child; he calls himself a Balu-man; has learned the Mendi language since he was a slave; 5 ft. 6 in. in height.

(8.) **Kwong** was born at Mam-bui, a town in the Mendi country. When a boy he was called Ka-gnwaw-ni. Kwong is a Bullom name. He was sold by a Timmani gentleman in the Du-bu country, for crim. con. with his wife, to Luisi, a Spaniard, at Lomboko. He is in middle life, 5 ft. 6 in. high.

No. 9.   No. 10.   No. 11.

(9.) **Fu-li-wa,** Fu-li, (*sun,*) called by his fellow prisoners Fuliwa, (*great Fuli*) to distinguish him from Fu-li-wu-lu, (*little Fuli,*) was born at Ma-no, a town in the Mendi country, where his king, *Ti-kba,* resided. He lived with his parents, and has five brothers. His town was surrounded by soldiers, some were killed, and he with the rest were taken prisoners. He passed through the Vai country, when taken to Lomboko, and was one month on the journey. He is in middle life, 5 ft. 3 in. high, face broad in the middle, with a slight beard. It was this Fuli who instituted the suit against Ruiz and Montez.

(10.) **P-ie,** *Pi-e,* or *Bi-a,* (5 ft. 4½ in. high,) calls himself a Timmani, and the father of Fu-li-wu-lu. He appears to have been distinguished for hunting in his country: says he, has killed 5 leopards, 3 on the land, and 2 in the water; has killed three elephants. He has a very pleasant countenance; his hands are whitened by wounds received from the bursting of a gun barrel, which he had overloaded when showing his dexterity. He had a leopards skin hung up on his hut, to show that he was a hunter. He has a wife and four children. He recognizes with great readiness the Timmani words and phrases contained in Winterbottom's account of Sierra Leone. He and his son, seemed overjoyed to find an American who could articulate the sound of their native tongue.

No. 12.   No. 13.   No. 14.

(11.) Pu-gnwaw-ni, [**Pung-wu-ni,**] (*a duck,*) 5 ft. 1 in. high, body tatooed, teeth filed, was born at Fe-baw, in Sando, between Mendi and Konno. His mother's broth-

while the U.S. District Court, again led by Judge Judson, would decide the property and salvage issues.

In Circuit Court

The trial in circuit court began with a dramatic scene. The defense team asked the court for a writ of *habeas corpus* for the three girls. A writ of *habeas corpus* is a legal document that protects the accused from illegal imprisonment. This writ, if granted, would have forced the prosecution to present a compelling reason, such as strong evidence of wrongdoing, for imprisoning the girls. If none could be given, then the girls would have to be freed.

The defense team and the abolitionists desperately wanted this writ. It would free the children because there was no evidence that they had committed a crime. Also, a writ would give the children, and perhaps eventually all of the blacks, the same legal rights that whites enjoyed in court. Obtaining this status for blacks would be a major victory for the abolitionists' cause, for it would set an example that could be used in future cases involving blacks.

The abolitionists also wanted a writ because this would allow them to present all kinds of evidence in the defendants' interest as well as information about the abolitionists' crusade in general. The defense team had located several Africans who were sailors on ships docked in New York's harbor. Even though these men could not speak the Mende language well, they could understand enough of what the captives said to be able to do some interpreting for them. The abolitionists were certain that if their story could be told, the Africans' testimony would strike a real blow at slavery. Not only would it publicly expose the horrors of the practice in a way few blacks had ever been able to do, it would allow the abolitionists to once again argue that such horrors would continue until the demand for slaves was eliminated. This, of course, would only happen when slavery was abolished everywhere.

District Attorney Holabird objected vehemently to the request for a writ. Holabird argued that the only question before the court was who should have jurisdiction over the trial, Spain or the United States. Besides, writs of *habeas corpus* were only issued for people, Holabird said with a sneer, and slaves were nothing more than property. And, he added, he could cite plenty of court cases to back his argument. This was a true statement; many American courts had declared that slaves were property without any legal rights.

As soon as Holabird sat down, Baldwin rose to his feet and asked the U.S. marshal to bring in the three little girls, who were between seven and nine years of age. All three eyed the spectators with great apprehension. As the marshal led them into the room, the girls, who expected the worst, burst into tears and clung to the marshal for protection. Baldwin pointed to the little girls, wondering aloud if the observers in the courtroom could truly see them as nothing more than property.

But the prosecution wasn't about to be swayed by tears. For two days it argued against the defense's pleas for a writ. Tempers flared repeatedly as each side challenged the other's statements. There was much at stake.

Then, on the third day of the trial, the prosecution stunned the courtroom by taking a new position. Holabird argued that no writ was necessary because the prisoners were not slaves but free men after all and should be returned to Africa. Apparently Holabird had decided that the only way he could avoid the damage that courtroom testimony might cause President Van Buren was to get the captives out of the country. If he couldn't send them to Cuba, then Africa would do.

Justice Thompson, taken aback by the prosecution's change in tactics, asked both sides to present the rest of their evidence in writing. This would prevent either side from drastically altering its case again. Thompson also said that he intended to take several days to study the facts.

On the morning of September 23, Thompson announced his decisions before a hushed courtroom. The United States could not try the captives for murder or piracy since the revolt had clearly taken place on a Spanish ship in Spanish-controlled waters. This was a major victory for the Africans as long as they could remain outside the grasp of the Spanish.

But the defense lawyers did not receive their writ. Thompson refused to order one because the question of whether or not the captives were free men or property had not been determined, and claims for them as property were before an American court.

On Trial in the District Court

Judge Judson then called the district court to order. The abolitionists would greatly have preferred another officer. Judson, before he became a judge, had led the legal crusade against his neighbor Prudence Crandall when she included black girls in her school in Canterbury, Connecticut.

Judson began his session by announcing that the first thing that had to be determined was the exact location of the *Amistad* when it was seized. This information would decide whether or not the case belonged in a Connecticut courtroom. Judson then closed the session, giving all sides until November 19 to prepare their cases.

Baldwin asked Judson to allow bail for the captives. However, when Judson announced that the fee set had to be the equivalent of what each captive would bring as a slave, the abolitionists refused to put up bail, believing that to do so would be the same as admitting that a price could be put on a human being.

As a compromise, Judson instructed the jailers to stop treating the Africans as if they were criminals, since no court had found them guilty of anything. Cinque was to be allowed to join the other African men. In addition, the men were to be given some time outside each day, so that they could exercise in fresh air and sunshine. The children were to be taken from the jail and housed in a private home. Later, the men would be moved to a house outside New Haven, where they would enjoy more privacy, space, and freedom.

In the Meantime

While the lawyers prepared their arguments, the *Amistad* Committee once again turned its attention to finding a good interpreter. Professor Josiah Gibbs of nearby Yale University finally discovered a Mende sailor, James Covey, working on a British ship in New York's harbor. Gibbs rushed Covey to New Haven to talk to the captives. Although Cinque was at first hesitant to trust the interpreter, the others were overjoyed at being able to tell what had happened to someone who could understand them.

Now that the language barrier had been broken, some students from Yale visited the jail. They were intent upon teaching the captives English while they were imprisoned. Understanding English would enable the Africans to speak for themselves without an interpreter. It would also make it possible for divinity students to try to convert the blacks to Christianity, and many of the lessons of the day, which often ran four or five hours long, included Bible studies.

A further boost to the captives' cause came from an Englishman, Dr. Richard Madden, who had lived in Cuba for many years. He had come to the United States to testify after hearing about the *Amistad* case. Because Madden could not stay in America for very long, he gave sworn statements before Judge Judson that could be used in the November trial. Madden testified that 25,000 Africans were brought into Cuba each year aboard slave ships. Even more significant, he insisted that Spanish officials were well aware of the practice.[10]

Ruiz and Montes Are Arrested

Whether it was done to create more publicity or to punish the culprits, the defense team decided to charge Ruiz and Montes with false imprisonment on behalf of Cinque. Both Spaniards, who all along had known that the captives were not already Cuban slaves, were arrested and jailed in New York on October 17. When offered bail, Ruiz indignantly refused it, hoping instead to gain sympathy by remaining in jail. Montes, however, paid his fee and promptly grabbed the next ship to Cuba, never to be heard from again in the United States.

Needless to say, the Spanish foreign minister was enraged by the latest arrests. Why, he repeatedly asked Van Buren, couldn't he do something about a case that was getting more and more out of control every day?

January 1840

Although the case before Judson was supposed to be heard in November, it was postponed due to the illness of the interpreter. The district court didn't resume until January 7, 1840. Even though several months had passed since the last session, interest in the case had not dwindled. As before, the courtroom was packed.

One of the major attractions was Cinque, who was scheduled to testify. A local newspaper reporter had described Cinque as "one of those spirits that appear but seldom . . . possessing courage . . . accustomed to command,"[11] and he lived up to his publicity. Cinque, with the help of the interpreter Covey, told fascinated spectators his story, blow by blow. At one point, he even got down on the floor to demonstrate how the captives had been chained and then crammed into the ship's hold.

Judson continued to take testimony for five days. During this time, all claims for salvage and rewards were made.

At the same time, two ships waited nearby. One was the *Grampus,* sent by President Van Buren, who was now under tremendous pressure from the Spanish government. The *Grampus* was supposed to take the Africans to Cuba immediately if the court decided that they were indeed property. Once Cinque and the others were out of the country, the abolitionists could not appeal the decision.

The second ship had been outfitted by the abolitionists. If the captives lost their case in court, this vessel was supposed to take them to Canada, where they would be free. At least one member of the *Amistad* Committee worked with the

A Poem for Cinque

The plight of the Africans and the courage they displayed attracted the attention of many Americans. One abolitionist who was especially taken by Cinque's courage, well-known poet William Cullen Bryant, wrote a poem about the revolt's leader. This poem was published in the abolitionist newspaper, the *Emancipator,* on September 19, 1839, to coincide with Cinque's first day in court.

> Chained in a foreign land he stood,
>   A man of giant frame,
> Amid the gathering multitude
>   That shrunk to hear his name—
> All stern of look and strong of limb,
>   His dark eye on the ground—
> And silently they gazed on him
>   As on a *lion* bound.
>
> Vainly, but well, that chief had fought—
>   He was a captive now;
> Yet pride, that fortune humbles not,
>   Was written on his brow.
> The scars his dark broad bosom wore
>   Showed warrior true and brave;
> A prince among his tribe before,
>   *He could not be a slave.*

American Underground Railroad, smuggling into Canada slaves who had escaped from their owners. As a result, the Committee had enough connections and know-how to make the escape possible. How the abolitionists planned to get hold of the captives is not clear.

On January 13, Judge Judson announced his decision. The District Court of Connecticut was the proper court to hear the case, since Gedney, who technically captured the ship at high sea, could then take the ship to any port of his choice. Gedney was to receive one-third of the value of the *Amistad* and its cargo when it was sold. However, the judge stated, the captives were *not* part of the claim. They had been brought into Cuba illegally and according to the laws of Spain, these men and children were people, not property. They had revolted only to regain their freedom. Cinque and the others were to be taken back to Africa, their true home. Antonio, Ferrer's slave, was to be sent back to Cuba. Captain Green's claim for detaining the Africans on Long Island was denied.

Free at Last—Almost

When the verdict was announced, there was great joy among the captives, the abolitionists, and the defense team. This joy was short-lived, however, for within days after the verdict was announced, President Van Buren instructed Holabird to appeal the case. As the case worked its way through the appeals process, the judges continued to agree with Judson in the defense's favor. Finally, Holabird turned to the U.S. Supreme Court for relief. The Court agreed to hear the *Amistad* case in February, 1841. The battle royal was not over.

6.

Before the U.S. Supreme Court

As soon as the U.S. Supreme Court accepted the case, the *Amistad* Committee began to evaluate its chances of winning. Five of the justices on the Court were Southerners, including Chief Justice Roger Taney, and this made the Committee more than a little nervous. To strengthen their position, Committee members decided to ask a well-known, highly respected spokesperson to join the defense team. They selected John Quincy Adams.

Adams was the son of John Adams, the second president of the United States, and Abigail Adams, one of the first champions of women's rights in America. John Quincy had been encouraged to take a stand early in life by both of his parents, and as a result, he had made quite a reputation for

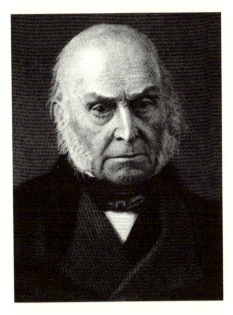

JOHN QUINCY ADAMS (1767–1848) had long been a political opponent of President Van Buren. Van Buren had made no secret of his dislike for Adams when Adams became president, and Van Buren, who was then governor of New York, openly attacked the president's policies. Engraving by W. Wellstood. Courtesy of the Dover Pictorial Archives.

himself as he fought for one of the greatest passions of his life—justice.

Adams was seventy-three years old when the *Amistad* Committee approached him, and by then he had acquired a great deal of political experience. He had represented Massachusetts in the U.S. Senate (1803–1808), served as a U.S. ambassador to several European countries, and had been President Monroe's secretary of state (1817–1825). It was during Monroe's term in office that Adams negotiated the Adams-Onis Treaty of 1819, one of the treaties that was constantly being referred to in the *Amistad* affair. John Quincy Adams had also been the sixth president of the United States (1825–1829). In 1840 when Baldwin asked him to help the

Committee, the former president was a member of the House of Representatives, where he had served his state for ten years. Adams was deeply opposed to slavery, but unlike the abolitionists, he thought that the practice should be ended gradually.

Even though he had been giving advice to the Committee whenever he had been asked to do so, Adams was reluctant to actually make a presentation on behalf of the *Amistad* captives. He argued that it had been more than thirty years since he had stood before the Court, and he really wondered if he was up to the challenge. Even so, the Committee insisted that they wanted him to join the defense team; his presence alone, they argued, would give prestige to the case. Shortly after his conversation with Baldwin, Adams began to prepare his arguments.

Presenting the Case

Due to several delays, the *Amistad* case was not heard until February 20, 1841, only a few weeks before a new president would be inaugurated. Van Buren had lost his re-election bid after all. Unlike trials in lower courts where witnesses testify and are cross-examined, arguments before the Supreme Court only involve the lawyers for the two sides.

The first person to address the Court was the Attorney General of the United States, Henry D. Gilpin, who had now replaced Felix Grundy. Gilpin spoke for almost two hours. He insisted that the United States had no choice but to return the blacks to Havana. The passports, he argued, had to be accepted as legitimate because the United States did not have the authority to question another country's papers. He then challenged Dr. Madden's testimony about the large number of illegal slaves in Cuba, labeling everything Madden had said as nothing more than hearsay. He concluded by referring to the treaties of 1795 and 1819, which agreed to return ships in distress, complete with their cargo, to their home ports. Since the papers were in order, Gilpin stated, this cargo included the captives.

Roger Sherman Baldwin then spoke for the Africans. His comments took the rest of the day as well as a portion of the Court's time the following morning. After telling Cinque's dramatic story, Baldwin hammered away at the attorney general's arguments. First, Baldwin insisted that the United States had every right to question the *Amistad*'s papers before taking any action for which it would be held accountable in the eyes of the world.

Next, he turned his attention to the treaties that the attorney general and the Spanish minister were so fond of citing. Baldwin pointed out that these treaties required proof of ownership before any property was to be returned. Baldwin told the Court that he had repeatedly challenged Ruiz and Montes to come to the courtroom to prove that the captives had been slaves in Cuba. The Spaniards had more than a year to do so, he added, and to date they still hadn't presented one shred of evidence that the slaves had lived and worked in Cuba for even a single day, let alone nineteen or more years.

Third, Baldwin presented arguments about the federal government's power, or more specifically, its lack of power. Baldwin argued that since Cinque and the others were free when they arrived in America, the federal government could not send them back to Cuba as slaves without violating the U.S. Constitution. The federal government, he reminded the justices, had no power to enslave anyone. Only the states could do this, and the case was no longer in a state court.

On February 24, John Q. Adams addressed the Court on behalf of the captives. He lacked confidence and said later that as he rose to present his case, he felt "deeply distressed and agitated."[12] Once Adams began to speak, however, he began to feel more in control of himself and his case. Adams reinforced many of Baldwin's arguments, adding some new insights as he went along. For example, Adams argued that the Adams-Onis Treaty was never meant to apply in cases such as this one, and he assured the Court that such issues were never discussed when he and Onis drafted the treaty. Also, this treaty was meant to deal with ships in distress in *wartime*, a fact that the government had completely ignored.

Then Adams added a new twist. He had been enraged by President Van Buren's interference in this case, and he now argued that this interference presented a great danger to the courts. Adams discussed copies of incriminating letters and orders, which he had obtained as a member of the House of Representatives, including the request for the *Grampus* to take the captives to Cuba so that the abolitionists couldn't appeal the decision. He even pointed to documents that had clearly been altered before being given to Congress for examination. Adams was incensed by the fact that the president of the United States had attempted to deny the blacks their legal rights.

Because of the president's involvement, Adams asked the Court to reverse part of the district court's decision that turned the captives over to the president for their return to Africa. Adams didn't trust Van Buren. He suspected that if the president became responsible for the Africans' return to Sierra Leone, they might be "intercepted" by a Spanish vessel and never reach their destination.

While the justices continued to watch his every move, Adams lectured the Court for four hours. If the justices gave in to the president's demands, Adams thundered, they would be responsible for a great injustice. In addition, the Court would be setting a dangerous precedent. From then on, any president could expect the justices to do his bidding whenever the lower courts failed to do so. And then, Adams wondered aloud, how safe would anyone's rights be?

Justice Story spoke for all the justices when he described

this remarkable scene later in a letter to his wife. He thought that Adams's argument was "extraordinary—extraordinary, I say, for its power and its bitter sarcasm and its dealing with topics far beyond the record and points of discussion."[13]

Adams gave one more four-hour presentation later to sum up the position of the defense. When he was finished, the captives and their lawyers began the long wait for the Court's decision. Once it was delivered, it would mean the end of the courtroom battles. There were no other courts in which to appeal.

The Court's Decision

On March 9, Justice Joseph Story announced the justices' decision. The blacks, he said, were free. He ruled that neither Ruiz and Montes nor the Spanish government had proved that the captives had been slaves in Cuba. Furthermore, Story said, the treaties that had been quoted so often did not apply in this case, just as Adams had insisted. The justice continued by pointing out that all human beings have a right to fight for their freedom. Even if the captives had committed dreadful acts, they had done so only because they had no other choice; therefore, they should not be punished.

As soon as Story had finished his comments, Adams rushed to a desk to write a note to Baldwin, who was not able to be present that day.

Roger S. Baldwin, Esq. New Haven
Washington. Tuesday, 9 March 1841. Noon

Dear Sir,
    The decision of the Supreme Court in the case of the
Amistad has this moment been delivered by Judge Story.
The captives are free. . . .
    The rest of the decisions of the courts below, including
Lieutenant Gedney's claim for salvage, affirmed. . . .
    Yours in great haste and great joy.

J. Q. Adams[14]

Reactions

When word of the decision finally reached the captives in Connecticut—and this took time in a day and age when telephones and television didn't exist—the Africans were understandably skeptical. After all, they had been declared free before and then locked up. It was hard for them to believe that their legal ordeal was finally over.

The abolitionists, however, were eager to embrace the decision. They rushed to publicize the outcome in books and pamphlets and lectures. They even printed several thousand copies of Baldwin's arguments in court and distributed them to anyone who showed interest in the case. Abolitionist newspapers, including committee member Leavitt's paper, the

Kali's Letter

The Africans had a difficult time understanding why they were imprisoned. Before the Supreme Court hearing, one of the children, Kali, wrote to John Quincy Adams, to ask for freedom. Although the boy's English is not perfect, no one could mistake his pain and frustration or his desire for freedom.

Dear Friend Mr. Adams:

I want to write a letter to you because you love Mende people, and you talk to the grand court. We want to tell you one thing. Jose Ruiz say we born in Havana, he tell lie. . . . We all born in Mende [country]. . . .

We want you to ask the Court what we have done wrong. What for Americans keep us in prison? Some people say Mende people crazy; Mende people dolt [stupid] because we no talk America language. Merica people no talk Mende language; Merica people dolt?

They tell bad things about [us] and we no understand. Some [visitors] say [we are] very happy because [we] laugh and have plenty to eat. Mr. Pendleton [the jailer] come, and [we] all look sorry because [we] think about Mende land and friends we no see now. Mr. Pendleton say [we look] angry; white men afraid of [us]. [We] no look sorry again—that why we laugh. But [we] feel sorry; O, we can't tell how sorry. . . .

ONE OF THE MOST POPULAR CAPTIVES in the public's eye was young Kali. This portrait was drawn by William H. Townsend in 1839. Courtesy of the Beinecke Rare Book and Manuscript Library, Yale University.

Dear friend Mr. Adams, you have children, you have friends, you love them, you feel very sorry if Mende people come and carry them all to Africa. We feel bad for our friends, and our friends all feel bad for us. . . . If American people give us free we glad, if they no give us free we sorry—we sorry for Mende people little, we sorry for American people great deal, because God punish liars. We want you to tell court that [we] no want to go back to Havana; we no want to be killed. Dear Friend, we want you to know how we feel. Mende people think, think, think. Nobody know what we think. . . . All we want is make us free.[15]

Emancipator, called the decision a great victory. Not only had it saved thirty-five blacks from becoming slaves, it had proved that blacks could get justice in an American court.

Making Plans

When the celebrations were over, it was time for the Africans to make plans to go home. The Court had not assigned the former captives to the president for their return voyage to Africa, just as Adams had requested. This meant that the captives or the abolitionists would have to make the necessary arrangements.

In the meantime, the Africans were staying on a farm owned by an abolitionist in Farmington, Connecticut. Here the men lived in a dormitory-like building. The children remained in private homes. To help raise money for the voyage, the abolitionists bought materials for craft projects so that the men could make and sell African handicrafts. The *Amistad* Committee also made arrangements for the Africans to give presentations to local churches and abolitionist groups. These programs raised large sums of money, and they drew lots of attention to the cause of abolition.

The Committee wanted the Africans to remain in the United States for several years to speak out against slavery and to learn as much about Christianity as they could so that they could serve as teachers and missionaries when they reached their homeland. But after six months, it became clear that to keep the Africans in America any longer would be cruel. They desperately wanted to go home now, and many were depressed again. One of the men, Foni, became so despondent that he committed suicide. The Mendes believed that their souls would live in Mende country after death, and Foni was convinced that the only way he would ever see his beloved Africa again was to die. Shortly after his death, the abolitionists decided to make preparations for the Africans' voyage to Sierra Leone as quickly as possible. The end of the ordeal was in sight at last.

Afterword

B<small>Y</small> N<small>OVEMBER</small> 1841, *Amistad* Committee members, with the help of abolitionists throughout the country, had made the necessary arrangements for the Africans to return to Sierra Leone. Members had chartered a ship, the *Gentleman,* and raised enough money to finance five missionaries in Africa: Reverend and Mrs. William Raymond, Reverend James Steele, and two black teachers who had taught the captives, Mr. and Mrs. Henry Wilson.

On November 25, the Africans prepared to board the *Gentleman* as friends and supporters gathered to say farewell. Cinque and Kali, who had spoken to numerous churches in the area as part of their fund-raising efforts, had touched the hearts of many congregational members with their stories. Now these members hovered about for one last glimpse of the former captives, presenting small gifts to the Africans so that they might remember their friends in America. After Lewis Tappan spoke to the Africans and Cinque thanked the Committee once more for all it had done during the last two years, everyone knelt and prayed together one more time. It was an emotional scene that brought tears to many eyes.

Africa!

In January 1842, after a thankfully uneventful voyage, thirty-five of the original fifty-three mutineers arrived in Freeport, Sierra Leone. Cinque and the others were among a very small number of slaves who ever saw their homeland again, and their gratitude and relief was evident in a letter to Lewis Tappan written by Kinna.

> We have reached Sierra Leone . . . and we land very safely. Oh dear friend . . . we will pray for you. . . . We have been on great water. Not any danger fell upon us. . . . Dear Mr. Tappan, how I feel for these wonderous things. . . . If I never see you in this world, we shall meet in heaven.[16]

The Americans were eager to start their Christian mission, which would include a school and a church, as soon as possible. This mission was to be built in Cinque's homeland, and after a brief rest from the long voyage, the group began to

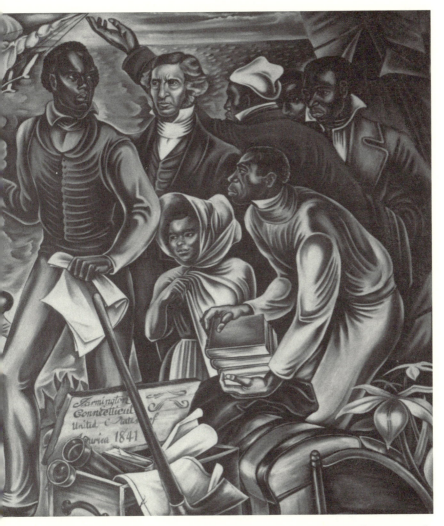

THE CAPTIVES' ARRIVAL IN AFRICA was an emotional event. Cinque stands in the center, holding a paper in his left hand. Former captives and American missionaries surround him. Mural by Hale Woodruff. Courtesy of Talladega College.

march toward Mende land. When they reached Cinque's village, they were told that it had been destroyed during a war with a rival tribe. Putting a mission there was no longer practical.

Cinque was devastated when he learned that no one had seen his wife or children recently. Surviving villagers believed they probably had been carried off and sold into slavery during the war. Some sources say he looked for his loved ones for many years, even traveling to the West Indies to see if he could find them there and buy their freedom. He was unsuccessful in his search, and, as he had feared the day that he was captured, he would never see any of them again.

The mission was set up on the coast and later relocated several times due to numerous problems. It was finally established on Sherbro Island, where it thrived.

Although the former captives had every intention of remaining at the mission, many slipped away as they ran into old friends or found that they could no longer resist the yearning to see their old homes again. Within a year, only the children and ten adults remained with the Americans. Eventually, even Cinque would leave.

The children continued their education at the mission. Margru, who showed special promise, was sent back to the U.S. to be educated at Oberlin College in Ohio, whose founders included Arthur Tappan, Lewis's brother. She became the principal of the mission's school when she returned to Africa.

In 1879, Cinque, who had often visited Sherbro, returned

to die there. He was given a Christian funeral and buried beside the mission.

The Spanish

As soon as Cinque and the rest of the mutineers were out of reach and the Spanish had no hope of getting them back, the Spanish government sought compensation for the captives and the *Amistad,* which was in such poor shape that it could not withstand a voyage to Cuba. Knowing that they couldn't get any satisfaction from the president or the courts, the Spanish turned their attention to the U.S. Congress. After some consultations, Southern senators passed a bill authorizing the government to pay Spain $50,000 for the loss of the captives and the ship. When this bill reached the House of Representatives, John Quincy Adams led the opposition. He argued that there was no reason to pay the Spanish anything. Besides, he added, to do so would be an insult to the Supreme Court. Although the bill was defeated, it wouldn't be the last time that the issue was raised. In fact, claims for compensation continued until the late 1850s.

The Abolitionists

In 1839, when the *Amistad* appeared near Long Island, slavery was regarded as an acceptable practice by the American public, just as it had been for almost two hundred years. By 1860, however, the abolitionists had gained many supporters in the North, and their goal of ending slavery in the United States was in sight. This incredible change in only twenty-one years was due to several dramatic events, in addition to incidents like the *Amistad* affair.

The first event was a war with Mexico between 1846 and 1848 in which the United States gained large tracts of land in the West. Southern members of Congress wanted this land and the states that would be carved from it to be open to slavery. If slavery were permitted in the new territories, slaveholders could move to better land further west. It would also increase the number of representatives in Congress who were friendly to slavery and would protect it. But Northern representatives, some of whom had long tolerated slavery in the South, objected to any expansion of it.

As a result, debates about this issue in Congress eventually became so heated that they turned into shouting matches. Even though it was extremely difficult to do so, Congress managed to work out a compromise in 1850 that would admit one slave state into the Union for each non-slave state. This compromise shocked many Americans who believed that slavery was destined to die out, and it enraged the abolitionists, who didn't want one more inch of slave territory in the United States, let alone more slave states.

Another attempt at compromise in 1854, the Kansas-Nebraska Act, kept the issue before the public. When violent clashes between proslavery and antislavery groups took place in Kansas, the abolitionists made the most of it, arguing that slavery promoted hatred and violence, and as a result, it had to be eliminated.

Another dramatic event that affected Americans' attitude about slavery was the United States' attempt to obtain Cuba. In 1848, Spain turned down an offer of $100 million for the island. More offers were made over the years, all of which were rejected. Spain's refusal to sell Cuba distressed several American officials who recommended that the United States take the island by force. When this recommendation became known, every antislavery person—as well as every person opposed to war—was aghast! How, these people asked, could anyone suggest that the country go to war to acquire another slave state, no matter how rich its resources? This incident created a great deal of resentment in the North toward the South.

A third event, the publication of *Uncle Tom's Cabin* by Harriet Beecher Stowe in 1852, further upset the public. Stowe's novel showed what the life of a slave was like, and it was not a pretty picture. More than one million copies of her book were sold by 1860, and thousands more saw the play by G.L. Aiken that was created from the book. Now Americans began to question both the expansion of slavery, as well as the practice itself. Maybe, more and more Americans began to think, slavery was wrong, just as the abolitionists said.

The old *Amistad* Committee was soon absorbed into a new abolitionist organization, the Union Missionary Society, which in turn merged with others in 1846 to form The American Missionary Association. This group agreed to support the mission in Africa and became one of the most powerful abolitionist organizations in America. Lewis Tappan was its treasurer.

In addition to alerting the public to the evils of slavery, the abolitionists also sought political power so that they could change the laws and make slavery illegal. In 1840, the abolitionists founded the Liberty Party. Although this party's candidate for president got less than 7,000 votes in 1840, in 1844 he received more than 62,000 votes. This was a significant increase, but it was still far short of a majority of the country's more than 2 million voters.

So the party reorganized, joining with other Americans who opposed slavery. Known as the Free Soil Party, this organization chose former president Martin Van Buren as its candidate for president and Charles Francis Adams, John Q. Adams's son, as its vice-presidential candidate.

Van Buren had little chance of winning. From the beginning, he was haunted by charges that he had tried to influence the courts in the *Amistad* affair. Also, although the abolitionists were gaining strength, they still didn't have enough support to win the election. Even so, the Free Soil Party managed to poll almost 300,000 votes.

The Free Soilers would field a candidate one more time in 1852. He failed to win, but the party's ideals and principles were picked up by a new political organization on the scene, the Republican Party, which ran its first candidate in 1856. Abraham Lincoln was the party's second candidate, and slavery was a major issue during the 1860 election.

Southerners felt very threatened by the abolitionists, and Southern leaders feared that the whole North had joined their cause and meant to end slavery in the South—by force if necessary. This fear seemed well-founded when many Northerners cheered abolitionist John Brown's raid on a federal arsenal at Harpers Ferry, Virginia, in 1859. Brown and his followers tried to seize weapons to arm slaves for an all-out rebellion.

In addition, Southern states saw no way to solve the many problems that existed between the agricultural South and the industrialized North. As a result, Southern states voted to secede, or leave the Union, in 1860 in order to protect their way of life. They formed a new nation and assigned troops to protect its borders.

President Lincoln then ordered his troops to force these states back into the Union to keep the country together. The result was the long and bloody Civil War in which 600,000 men lost their lives. At its end, the slaves were freed.

Historians have long argued about the causes of the Civil War, and there is no agreement where slavery ranks among the many issues that divided the nation. Historians do agree, though, that this particular issue caused great friction between the North and South. Historians also agree that the issue would never have been in the spotlight as much as it was without the abolitionists' crusade.

Once the American slaves were free, the American Missionary Association began an extensive program to educate blacks in America. The association established schools throughout the South, including some famous institutions such as Talladega College, Fisk University, Dillard University, Tougaloo College, and Atlanta University. This society is still very active, and it continues to support some of these schools.

Pedro Blanco

While the abolitionists struggled to end slavery in America, the British set out to end Pedro Blanco's slave trade. Shortly after the *Amistad* case became a popular topic, British patrol ships raided the island and shut down Blanco's operation. Blanco, however, managed to escape, and because he was by then a very wealthy man, he was able to live out the rest of his life in luxury.

Interestingly enough, the Spanish—and especially the Cubans, who had for so long insisted that slaves were not being brought from Africa to Cuba—were nearly hysterical when they found out that Blanco's fort would no longer supply them with workers. Cuba's economy depended on slave labor, and since the incredibly hard work in the fields literally killed many workers, a constant supply of new slaves was needed if plantation owners were to continue to enjoy their wealthy lifestyle.

Antonio

And finally, although the Supreme Court ordered the return of Antonio, Captain Ferrer's slave, to Cuba, he, too, was freed. The abolitionists spirited him away to Canada, where he found work in Montreal. Clearly, the *Amistad* revolt had far-reaching effects on many lives, effects that Cinque and the other captives could not possibly have imagined as they fought for their freedom on that hot summer night in 1839 aboard the *Amistad*.

Notes

1. Robert Liston, *Slavery in America: The History of Slavery* (New York: McGraw-Hill, 1970), p. 17.

2. Robert Liston, *Slavery in America: The History of Slavery* (New York: McGraw-Hill, 1970), p. 33.

3. John Hope Franklin, *An Illustrated History of Black Americans* (New York: Time, 1970), p.17.

4. Bernice Kohn, *The Amistad Mutiny* (New York: McCall, 1971), pp. 3–4.

5. John W. Barber, "A History of the *Amistad* Captives," *Journal of the New Haven Colony Historical Society* 36 (Spring 1990), pp. 38–39.

6. John W. Barber, "A History of the *Amistad* Captives," *Journal of the New Haven Colony Historical Society 36* (Spring 1990), p. 39.

7. Howard Jones, *Mutiny on the Amistad* (New York: Oxford University Press, 1987), p. 48.

8. Howard Jones, *Mutiny on the Amistad* (New York: Oxford University Press, 1987), p. 48.

9. Howard Jones, *Mutiny on the Amistad* (New York: Oxford University Press, 1987), p. 49.

10. John W. Barber, "A History of the *Amistad* Captives," *Journal of the New Haven Colony Historical Society* 36 (Spring 1990), p. 50.

11. Helen Kromer, *The Amistad Revolt, 1839: The Slave Uprising Aboard the Spanish Schooner* (New York: Franklin Watts, 1973), p. 55.

12. Howard Jones, *Mutiny on the Amistad* (New York: Oxford University Press, 1987), p. 176.

13. Marie B. Hecht, *John Quincy Adams: A Personal History of an Independent Man* (New York: William Morrow, 1970), p. 582.

14. Bernice Kohn, *The Amistad Mutiny* (New York: McCall, 1971), p. 86.

15. Helen Kromer, *The Amistad Revolt, 1839: The Slave Uprising Aboard the Spanish Schooner* (New York: Franklin Watts, 1973), pp. 63–64.

16. Clifton Johnson, "The *Amistad* Case and Its Consequences in U.S. History," *Journal of the New Haven Colony Historical Society* 36 (Spring 1990), p. 19.

Bibliography

Barber, John Warner. "A History of the *Amistad* Captives." *Journal of the New Haven Colony Historical Society* 36 (Spring 1990): 32–64.

Dillon, Merton L. *The Abolitionists: The Growth of a Dissenting Minority.* DeKalb: Northern Illinois University Press, 1974.

Fishel, Leslie H., Jr., and Benjamin Quarles. *The Black American: A Documentary History.* New York: William Morrow, 1970.

Franklin, John Hope. *An Illustrated History of Black Americans.* New York: Time, 1970.

Hecht, Marie B. *John Quincy Adams: A Personal History of an Independent Man.* New York: Macmillan, 1972.

Howard, Thomas, ed. *Black Voyage: Eyewitness Accounts of the Atlantic Slave Trade.* Boston: Little, Brown, 1971.

Johnson, Clifton H. "The *Amistad* Case and Its Consequences in

U.S. History." *Journal of The New Haven Colony Historical Society* 36 (Spring 1990): 3–22

Jones, Howard. *Mutiny on the Amistad.* New York: Oxford University Press, 1987.

Kohn, Bernice. *The Amistad Mutiny.* New York: McCall, 1971.

Kolchin, Peter. *American Slavery: 1619–1877.* New York: Hill and Wang, 1993.

Kromer, Helen. *The Amistad Revolt, 1839: The Slave Uprising Aboard the Spanish Schooner.* New York: Franklin Watts, 1973.

Liston, Robert. *Slavery in America: The History of Slavery.* New York: McGraw-Hill, 1970.

McCain, Diana R. *Free Men: The Amistad Revolt and the American Anti-Slavery Movement.* New Haven, Conn: New Haven Historical Society, 1990.

Motley, Constance Baker. "The Legal Aspects of the *Amistad* Case." *Journal of the New Haven Colony Historical Society* 36 (Spring 1990): 23–31.

For More Information

The Amistad Revolt—"All We Want Is Make Us Free" is a 33-minute, full-color video accompanied by a 34-page teacher's guide, titled *Free Men.* Narrated by actress Vinie Burrows and taped at Connecticut's Mystic Seaport, a re-created nineteenth-century village, this drama of historical visuals, original score, and the voices of actors will galvanize the interest of all viewers from middle school age on up. Produced by the *Amistad* Committee, New Haven, Connecticut, it is available from Linnet Books, 2 Linsley Street, North Haven, Connecticut 06473.

Many slave rebellions took place over the years in addition to the *Amistad* revolt. For more information about such rebellions, read *Rebels Against Slavery: American Slave Revolts* by Patricia C. and Fredrick L. McKissack (New York: Scholastic, 1996).

To learn more about the triangular trade, see Clifford Lindsey

Alderman's book, *Rum, Slaves and Molasses: The Story of New England's Triangular Trade* (New York: Crowell-Collier Press, 1972). This book goes into detail about the trade, and it shows how much merchants and plantation owners depended upon it.

African Slavery (New York: Abelard-Schuman, 1973) by Edwin P. Hoyt gives more information about how slaves were captured. This text also describes what the slave forts, such as Lomboko, were like.

In Their Own Words: A History of the American Negro 1619– 1865 (New York: Thomas Y. Crowell, 1964), edited by Milton Meltzer, gives firsthand accounts of what it was like to be a slave. The slaves' stories include details about slave ships, Nat Turner's revolt, and slave auctions.

To learn more about the slaves' traumatic journey across the Atlantic Ocean, see Tom Feelings's book, *The Middle Passage* (Dial, 1995). Feelings tells his story using as few words as possible, relying instead on powerful illustrations to convey the horrors of the crossing.

And finally, for more information about Sierra Leone in the 1800s, check out a copy of Mary Louise Clifford's *The Land and People of Sierra Leone* (Philadelphia: J.B. Lippincott Company, 1974). Chapters two, three, four, and five discuss the slave trade and the establishment of colonies for freed slaves. There are numerous references to the Mende people.

Acknowledgments

THE AUTHOR AND PUBLISHER wish to thank Mr. Clifton H. Johnson, first executive director of The *Amistad* Research Center, New Orleans, for his help with this book. Mr. Al Marder, chair of The *Amistad* Committee, Inc., and Mr. Robert Egleston, executive director of The New Haven Colony Historical Society, both of New Haven, Connecticut, have also been valuable resources to the project.

Index